This book is in honor of Sir Peter Wright and for Julia and David

First published in Canada in 1995 by
Scholastic Canada Ltd.,
123 Newkirk Road, Richmond Hill, Ontario, Canada L4C 3G5

Photographs (c) 1995 Leslie E. Spatt
Copyright (c) 1995 Breslich & Foss

Conceived and produced by Breslich & Foss, London
Designer: Margaret Sadler
Editor: Laura Wilson

Canadian Cataloguing in Publication Data

    Spatt, Leslie E.
         The Sleeping beauty : behind the scenes
    at the ballet

ISBN 0-590-24536-8

1. Sleeping beauty (Choreographic work) — Juvenile literature. 2. Dance production — Juvenile literature. I. Title.

GV1790 .S8S63 1995   j792.8'42   C95-930137-2

First printing

Origination by Dot Gradations
Printed and bound in China

The author would like to thank The Birmingham Royal Ballet for their help and cooperation.

Front jacket: Miyako Yoshida and Michael O'Hare of the Birmingham Royal Ballet

CONTENTS

THE STORY

Once upon a time there lived a King and Queen who had no children. When the Queen gave birth to a daughter, the King was overjoyed, and ordered an enormous party to be held for her christening. Among the guests were the fairies who were to be godmothers to the Princess, who was named Aurora.

Each fairy presented the Princess with gifts. The Lilac Fairy was just about to present her gift when there was a clap of thunder, and the evil fairy Carabosse flew into the room, enraged that she had not been invited to the party. She said, "Now you can hear my gift to your precious Princess! When she grows up, she will prick her finger on a spindle and fall down dead!" The Queen begged her to change her mind, but she refused. However, the Lilac Fairy stepped forward and said, "This is my gift to the Princess: she will prick her finger, but she will not die. She will fall into a deep sleep and be awakened by the kiss of a handsome Prince." Furious, Carabosse disappeared in a puff of smoke.

The King commanded that all the spindles in the kingdom be burned. The years passed peacefully until Aurora's sixteenth birthday, when the King gave a party for his daughter. She was a beautiful young girl, and many of her suitors came to the feast. She had just finished dancing with them when an old woman came up to her. "I have a birthday present for you," she said, and gave her a spindle. Aurora was enchanted, and danced about with her new gift.

Before the King and Queen could take the spindle away from her, she had pricked her finger and fallen to the ground. In triumph, the old woman threw off her disguise and revealed herself as Carabosse. But the Lilac Fairy waved her wand, sending the court into a deep sleep, and a thick hedge of thorns grew up around the castle, shielding it from view.

One day a hundred years later, Prince Florimund came hunting in the forest. He was miserable because he was engaged to marry a lady he did not love. The Lilac Fairy appeared to him and showed him a vision of Princess Aurora. Prince Florimund thought she was the loveliest girl he had ever seen; but every time he tried to touch her, she slipped from his grasp, and just as he thought he was about to hold her in his arms, she vanished. "How can I find her?" he asked the Lilac Fairy.

"I'll show you," she replied, and led the Prince through the wood and into the hedge of thorns. They parted for him, their sharp points turning to roses as he passed. The Prince came to the castle, where he found Aurora lying fast asleep. Enchanted by her beauty, he bent over and kissed her, waking her. When she awoke, the King and Queen and all the court woke up from their deep sleep, too.

The wedding of Florimund and Aurora was celebrated with splendor, and the Lilac Fairy came to give the couple her blessing.

THE 𝒫RINCIPAL CHARACTERS

PRINCESS AURORA

This is one of the hardest roles in the women's classical repertoire, traditionally danced by a principal. There is a lot of very difficult and physically demanding dancing to do, and the dancer must always look radiant and smiling, even if she is straining every muscle and feels exhausted. *The Sleeping Beauty* is a four-act ballet, and Princess Aurora is on stage in three of the acts. The name Aurora means "dawn."

PRINCE FLORIMUND

The name Florimund means "flower of the world," and the Prince is a very romantic character. The part is usually danced by a principal or senior soloist, but sometimes a junior member of the company will be given a chance to perform it. As the Prince appears only in two acts, it is not as tiring a part as a character who appears in all four acts of the ballet. For this reason, it is often the first big classical part a male dancer will be asked to perform.

CARABOSSE

Carabosse, the evil fairy, is almost always a "character part" which can be played by either a man or a woman. She is often played by a senior character dancer, a long-standing member of the company who has possibly danced roles like Princess Aurora. Carabosse is wicked, but, unlike the ugly sisters in *Cinderella*, she does not have to look hideous. In some productions she is beautiful, but she is usually accompanied by ugly gnomes and goblins who are her attendants.

THE LILAC FAIRY

The Lilac Fairy is the good fairy, and in this production, it is a "character part." However, in some other productions the role is danced by a senior soloist or principal wearing *pointe* shoes and a tutu. *The Sleeping Beauty* ballet was created in Russia, where lilac means "wisdom." The Lilac Fairy is normally dressed in a blue or purple, or perhaps lavender, costume, and her attendants are beautiful fairies.

IN THE
*S*TUDIO

A dancer's day usually begins around 10 a.m. with a class. All dancers attend class, because they need to warm up their muscles and prepare for the rehearsals ahead. Classes and rehearsals take place in the studio, a large room with full-length mirrors on the walls so that the dancers can watch themselves and correct any mistakes. All studios have wooden floors, because the surface on which dancers move must be springy, not rigid. As wooden floors are usually uneven or splintered, vinyl flooring is put on top. Large ballet companies put vinyl flooring on their home stage and take the same surface with them when they go on tour, because the dancers are used to it.

Below: Dancers warming up with *barre* exercises.

THE CLASS

Classes always begin with barre work. The barre is a long pole that may be either fixed horizontally to the wall (as shown on page 9), or set up in the middle of the studio. For these exercises, the dancers should rest their hands on the barre, without holding onto it tightly. The purpose of this work is for the dancers to warm up, stretch their muscles, find their center of balance, and generally prepare themselves for center work in class and in the rehearsals that follow.

In center work, the dancers do not use the barre for support but instead move around the studio, perhaps doing more difficult versions of the barre exercises. Then they move on to turns and jumps, beginning with *adagio* (slow) steps and finishing with *allegro* (quick) steps. It is traditional to thank the teacher and the pianist with applause at the end of the class.

Far left: Dancers doing center work: *arabesques* on pointe.

Left: After the barre, there is a few minutes' break. Some dancers change into different shoes for center work.

THE REHEARSAL

Class is normally followed by rehearsals. The dancers check the call sheets on the notice board to find out which rehearsals they are supposed to attend. During rehearsals, the dancers learn all the different steps of the ballet — not only the big set pieces such as *pas de deux*, but also the linking steps that will get them from one part of the stage to the other. They also learn where they are supposed to be onstage at any given time. The dancers know that they must be at a particular place at a specific point in the music, but they can't always rely on the music, because a full orchestra of different instruments does not sound anything like the studio's single piano. So to avoid losing their place, they often count. How much they need to count depends on the music. *The Sleeping Beauty* music is easy, but in some ballets the whole stage is full of dancers thinking, "One, two, three, four, five, six, seven, eight…" in order to keep their place in the music.

If the production is brand new, there may be as much as two or three months of rehearsals before the

Right: Rehearsing an *attitude* for Princess Aurora's solo in Act 3. This dancer is wearing a practice tutu over her leotard to help her get the feel of the costume she will be wearing for the performance.

Above: Rehearsing for the Rose Adagio (see page 31). The ballet master (the man on the right) is standing in for one of the princes, and the girl dancing the part of Princess Aurora is practicing taking their hands while remaining in position on pointe.

Right: Rehearsing the Prince and Princess's pas de deux from Act 3. This movement is called a "fish dive." When two dancers are doing a complicated pas de deux like this one, it is very important that they trust each other so that they can concentrate on dancing well and not worry about slipping or being dropped and perhaps hurt.

opening night. However, a ballet like *The Sleeping Beauty* is very well known and almost every dancer will have either learned some of it at ballet school or danced it before, so it does not take so long to rehearse.

During rehearsals, the dancers who have the central roles in the ballet work on how to show the personality of their characters. Narrative ballet is not only about dancing beautifully, it is also about showing a character's feelings to the audience. Because they do not speak, dancers must do this with their movements. For example, in Act 1 of *The Sleeping Beauty*, Princess Aurora must first look very happy because it is her birthday party and many princes have come to ask for her hand in marriage. Then she must show curiosity about the poor old woman and her strange gift, and bewilderment as the spell of the spindle begins to work. Finally, she must be terrified when the old woman tears off her cloak and reveals that she is the evil fairy Carabosse.

BACKSTAGE

In a large ballet company, there are a lot of different jobs to be done, and there are far more people working behind the scenes than dancing onstage. These backstage workers fall into two main groups: people who look after the dancers' costumes, shoes, makeup, hairdressing, and wigs; and people who look after the stage and everything that goes on it, such as the technical staff and the stage manager. Yet another group of people, such as the director, the teachers, and the publicity department, look after the running of the company, and the orchestra provides music.

WARDROBE DEPARTMENT

The wardrobe department has the job of making and repairing the dancers' costumes. The designer gives the costume designs to the wardrobe department and tells them which fabrics and trimmings should be used to make them. The people who make the costumes are called the "production wardrobe." The people who take care of and repair the costumes are called the "running wardrobe." Costumes may become worn out or rip, and they also need to be cleaned.

Above: Sewing a tutu. It takes around a day and a half and ten yards of net fabric to make a tutu, and much of the stitching has to be done by hand.

Left: The almost finished tutu skirt is joined to the bodice, which is still being fitted.

Principal dancers and soloists usually have costumes made especially for them if there is no costume that fits well. Dancers in the *corps de ballet* are given an existing costume which will fit them. Most costumes have several sets of fastenings at the back so that they can fit different people. Before each performance, the wardrobe assistants or dressers hang up the costumes on a rail in the dressing room so that they are ready for the dancers to wear. It is each dancer's job to check half an hour before the performance that everything needed for the costume is there. Normally female dancers wear pink or white tights, and male dancers wear whatever color the designer has chosen. The tights are dyed by the wardrobe department.

Right: Repairing a costume.

Below: Tutus hanging up. The word *tutu* is an old French word. It is slang for "bottom."

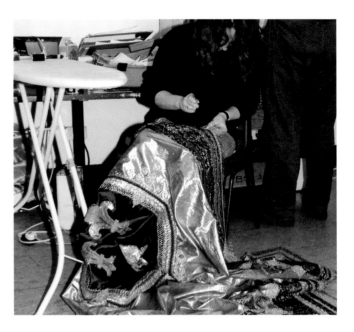

BALLET SHOES

Women's ballet shoes are made of canvas, leather, or satin, and kept on with elastic or with ribbons tied around the ankle. Dancers sew the ribbons onto the shoes themselves. Women's block-toed shoes are called *pointe* shoes (dancing on pointe means dancing on tiptoe). Pointe shoes are made of satin, with the fronts specially stiffened by glue. After a while, the glue softens and the shoes are no longer good enough to wear in an actual performance. When this happens, the dancers either re-stiffen the fronts using shellac, or keep the shoes to wear only in rehearsals and for class. Some dancers believe that a particular pair of shoes will bring them luck, so they keep on wearing them until they almost fall apart! Men's shoes are made of soft leather or canvas, and usually held on by elastic, although some male dancers sometimes glue their shoes onto their tights instead.

Ballet shoes are kept in a special shoe room backstage. Principal ladies are usually allowed up to twenty pairs of shoes every month, and those in the corps de ballet usually get ten pairs. Everyone has special little details they like their shoes to have.

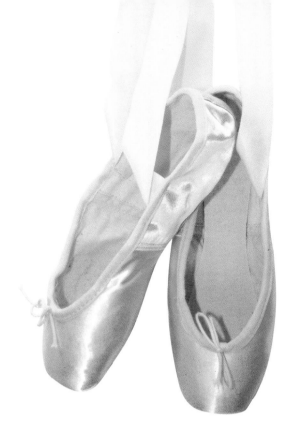

Below right: A dancer sews ribbons onto her shoes. The ribbons should be made of satin or nylon the same color as the shoe.

Below left: Ribbons should be knotted twice to make them secure, and the ends neatly tucked in — ends that stick out are called "pig's ears"!

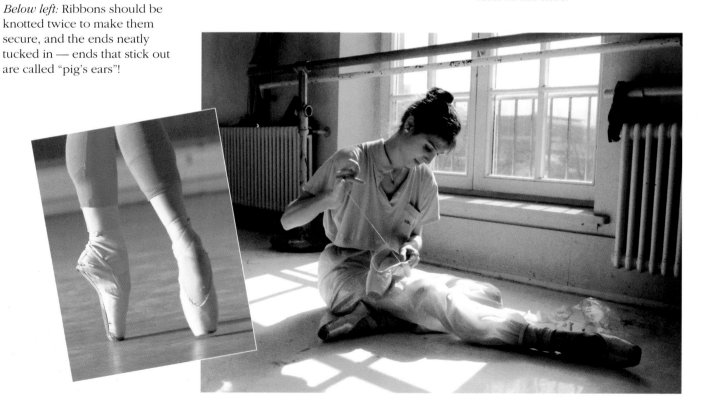

14

SUSAN LUCAS

RACHEL PEPPIN

JILLIAN MACKRILL

ANNETTE PAIN

Left: Pointe shoes being stored in the shoe room. Each dancer has her own cubbyhole.

MAKEUP AND HAIR

Most dancers prefer to do their own makeup, except when it is very complicated. Dancers use stage makeup, which they put on heavily so that everyone in the audience can see their faces. Sometimes the designer tells the dancers to do their makeup in a particular way to go with their costumes. Dancers' makeup is *always* applied before they put on their costumes. This is how one of the dancers in *The Sleeping Beauty* does her makeup and hair.

4. She applies eyeliner all around her eyes.

1. Using a makeup stick, she applies a base makeup all over her face.

5. She makes sure that the eyelashes are firmly in place.

2. She spreads the base makeup evenly with a sponge, making sure it blends in and does not leave a line under her chin.

6. She puts on some mascara so that the false eyelashes blend in with her real eyelashes.

3. She applies false eyelashes with glue.

7. Using the eyeliner, she draws a line across the top of the false eyelashes to hide the join.

16

8. She darkens her eyebrows with an eyebrow pencil.

9. She outlines her lips with a lip liner.

10. She fills in the outline with lipstick to finish her makeup.

11. She combs her hair and gathers it up into a high ponytail.

12. She makes it into a bun near the top of her head.

13. She checks in the mirror to make sure there are no loose ends of hair.

14. She puts on her headdress. To keep it on, there is a string on each side. She ties the strings together at the base of her hair.

15. She pins the strings in place with hair pins so that they will not slip.

DRESSING FOR THE PERFORMANCE

It is 6:30 p.m., and the changing rooms are packed with dancers preparing for the evening performance. After they have done their makeup and warmed up at the barre, the dancers put on their costumes. Tights are always put on first, followed by tutus for the women and shirts or tunics for the men, and lastly any outer pieces such as cloaks or swords.

Below: Princess Aurora adjusts the fastenings on her tutu.

Right: One of the wardrobe assistants hooks up a costume for Act 1.

Shoes are put on when the dancer prefers: some dancers like to add them before putting on their costumes, some afterward. Many of the dancers in this ballet have one or two costume changes during the performance.

Above: One of the fairies in the Prologue puts on her shoes. The violin and guitar are props for the court musicians in Act 2.

Right: There is no intermission between Acts 1 and 2, so these dancers have to do a very quick change. The dancer in the foreground is changing into a court musician's costume. He will grab one of the musical instruments shown above before he goes on stage for Act 2.

STAGE PREPARATION

It is half an hour before the curtain. The stagehands make sure that everything is in its proper place and that the scenery has been put up securely and will not fall over. If the ballet company is at home in its own theater, the dancers can warm up in the studio if they want, but if they are on tour and in a strange theater, a barre will be put onstage for them and they will warm up there. The stage manager gives a series of calls to tell the dancers how much time they have to get dressed and ready before the performance starts: a half-hour call, a fifteen-minute call, and a five-minute call. Then she says, "Beginners, please, onstage," so that the dancers who are first on the stage know that the curtain is about to be raised.

Below right: The stage manager sits at her control desk.

Below: The chief electrician checks that everything on the chandelier is working.

WARMING UP

Dancers do their warm-up exercises before putting on their costumes. Once their costumes are on, they usually practice some of the steps in their solos and keep themselves warm by pointing their feet or simple stretching and bending. They dip the toes of their shoes into the rosin box to make them grip the stage properly. This keeps the dancers from slipping.

Above: A dancer warming up at the barre.

Left: Keeping feet warm while waiting for the performance to start.

Below: The rosin box. These dancers are putting the heels of their tights (in addition to the toes of their shoes) into the rosin box to help keep their shoes securely on their feet.

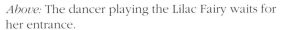

Above: The dancer playing the Lilac Fairy waits for her entrance.

Top right: The head of the running wardrobe department makes some last-minute adjustments to a costume.

Center right: The lighting engineer checks the lighting cues. Most of the lighting is controlled by computer, but the engineer raises and lowers the lights over the audience — known as the house lights — himself.

Below right: Dancers warming up in the last few minutes before the performance.

Above: Dancers warming up. The dancer on the right is taking a minute to think about her role and prepare herself for the coming performance. The warm-up barre will be removed just before the curtain is raised.

Right: Waiting in the wings. Dancers often stand in the wings to watch each other performing. If they will be dancing a particular part themselves later in the season, watching another dancer in the role can be helpful. If someone is dancing a role for the first time, the wings are usually crowded with dancers who want to watch and wish the dancer luck.

THE PERFORMANCE

THE PROLOGUE

The music begins and the curtain goes up to reveal the palace, where the christening celebration for the royal daughter, Princess Aurora, is about to take place. Catalabutte, the master of ceremonies, is in charge, and at his bidding courtiers with candles light up the room and make everything ready for the baby, who is carried in by her nurse, followed by the King and Queen.

Above: Catalabutte, with his staff of office, gives the orders.

Right: The King and Queen check the list of guests to make sure that no one has been forgotten.

Above: The fairies who are guests at the christening come onstage, with the Lilac Fairy coming last. They greet the King and Queen, who invite them to dance.

Left: The dance of the Lilac Fairy's attendants. Here they are doing arabesques.

Left: During the dance, the baby is brought into the midst of the fairies to be blessed.

Below: The Lilac Fairy's attendants weave through the solo fairies and the cavaliers who attend them.

Carabosse enters, furious that she has not been invited to the christening. She first turns to the King and, in mime, asks why she has been forgotten. The King blames his master of ceremonies, Catalabutte. Carabosse turns to Catalabutte, and, without saying a word, shows him exactly what she thinks of him. Then she announces, still in mime, "Now you will hear my gift to the Princess. She will grow up to be very beautiful, but she will prick her finger on a spindle and die!" The Queen begs her to change her mind, but Carabosse refuses.

Carabosse is a role that can be played by either a male or a female dancer. The dancers shown playing Carabosse in these two pictures are married to each other in real life!

Above: Drumrolls in the orchestra and lightning flashes onstage announce the arrival of Carabosse.

Right: Carabosse mimes the word *die*.

MIME

Many ballets make use of a special sign language, so that the dancers can "talk" to each other. In *The Sleeping Beauty*, both Carabosse and the Lilac Fairy need to use mime in order to tell an important part of the story. As you can see from the photographs here, this involves a very complicated sequence of actions. All the gestures of mime need to be very exaggerated, so that everyone in the audience is able to see them. After Carabosse has cursed the Princess Aurora, the Lilac Fairy steps forward. Here are some of the gestures she uses as she tells the court that she will save the Princess. The word she is miming is indicated in bold type.

3. You want to…

4. kill her.

1. The Lilac Fairy says, **I**…

2. love Princess Aurora.

5. Why?

Carabosse still insists that the Princess will die, so the Lilac Fairy tells the court, "Now you will hear my gift to Princess Aurora. She will prick her finger…"

6. but she will not die.

7. She will **fall asleep**…

8. and a **prince** will come…

9. and with a **kiss**…

10. he will **awaken** her!

The Lilac Fairy promises that Princess Aurora will not die from pricking her finger when she grows up. Carabosse rushes off in a rage, and the curtain falls as the court gathers around the baby Princess.

ACT 1

The curtain rises to show the palace garden. Sixteen years have passed, and Princess Aurora has grown into a beautiful young woman. The scene is set for another party — this time for Princess Aurora's birthday.

Below: The guests at the party do a dance that is called the Garland Dance because the women carry garlands of flowers.

THE GARLAND DANCE

In this version the dance is performed by twelve people: six men and six women. The women carry garlands of flowers and create patterns with them while they are dancing. During this, four princes who have been invited to the party come onstage. Each one hopes that he will marry Princess Aurora.

Many things in Act 1 must be danced similarly in every production in order to tell the story properly, but this dance gives the producer a chance to invent something that will be different and will happen only in his or her production of the ballet.

THE ROSE ADAGIO

⸺

This is a special dance for Princess Aurora and her four princes. She dances with each prince in turn, and they each give her a rose. This is why the dance is named the Rose Adagio. It is one of the most difficult pieces in the entire repertoire of the female dancer. For the last part of the dance, she must stand on pointe, without a break, while each prince takes her hand and promenades her in a circle. The princes must be very careful to take hold of her hand at exactly the right moment; otherwise she might lose her balance. Even if an Aurora sometimes wobbles, she must never come off pointe!

Below left: After the garland dance, Princess Aurora enters. Excited by the party, she leaps across the stage in a *grand jeté*.

Below right: The end of the Rose Adagio.

After the Rose Adagio, there is a dance for all Princess Aurora's young friends. The four princes ask Aurora to dance a solo for them, and she does so. Then her friends begin a lively dance, which she joins and then continues alone. As Aurora dances, carefree and happy, an old woman comes into the garden and makes her way toward the young Princess. She presents her with a bunch of flowers. When Aurora takes them, she discovers a strange object hidden in the flowers. She does not recognize that it is a spindle, and neither do any of her friends, because the King banned all the spindles from the kingdom after

Carabosse's curse. The Princess is enchanted by her present and refuses to be parted from it. She dances around the stage with it until she accidentally pricks her finger.

As the spell begins to work, the Princess feels faint but recovers herself and carries on dancing. Dizzy and confused, she spins around the stage until she falls to the ground. At this point, the old woman pulls off her disguise and reveals herself as the evil fairy Carabosse. She tells the court, "You remember what I said. She will prick her finger and she will die!" Then she disappears from the stage.

Above: Disguised as an old woman, Carabosse gives the spindle to Aurora.

Right: Amazed by this new gift, Aurora drops the flowers to examine the spindle more closely.

Opposite: The Queen holds the fainting Aurora in her arms.

The Lilac Fairy appears in Carabosse's place and tells the horrified King and Queen that their daughter is only sleeping and will not die. She tells the four princes to carry Aurora back to the castle. Then she puts a spell on the court so that they, too, will sleep until the Prince wakes Aurora.

Right: The Lilac Fairy casts a spell to put the court to sleep.

ACT 2

Ahundred years has passed. Prince Florimund and his intended bride, the Countess, are out hunting in the forest with a party of their friends. The Prince is bored and unhappy, because he is not sure if he loves his fiancée and really does not want to marry her.

After a series of solos and court dances, the Prince's tutor dashes onstage, saying, "I've seen the quarry. Let's go after it!" Prince Florimund's friends eagerly agree, but he hangs back. The Countess asks him if he will join them in the hunt, but he refuses, telling her to go ahead. He wants to remain behind. The entire party rushes off, leaving him alone. As he wanders about the stage, the music and lighting change to create a mood of mystery and enchantment. At first, the Prince wanders aimlessly, but then he senses that something strange is happening around him. Bewildered, he looks around, and sees the Lilac Fairy, who has appeared behind him onstage. In mime, she asks him, "Why are you here?"

"I don't know," replies the Prince.

"Why are you so unhappy?" asks the Lilac Fairy.

"I don't know that, either," says the Prince.

"Are you in love?"

Above: Prince Florimund looks on as his companions enjoy the hunting party.

Prince Florimund thinks for a moment and then admits, "No, I'm not in love."

"I will show you a beautiful woman," says the Lilac Fairy, and she shows him Princess Aurora, who appears as a vision behind one of the gauze curtains at the back of the stage.

The Prince gasps, "She's so beautiful! I love her!" But as he runs to the vision, it disappears. "Where has she gone?" he asks.

"Wait," replies the Lilac Fairy. "I will show you." She brings on her attendant nymphs, and as they dance, Aurora appears onstage in their midst. The nymphs retreat to the edges of the stage, leaving Prince Florimund gazing at Aurora.

Top: The Prince dancing with the Countess.

Right: The Lilac Fairy presents Aurora to the Prince.

Prince Florimund goes toward Aurora, but every time he approaches her, she either runs away from him or the nymphs draw him back. As he stands wondering what to do, Aurora suddenly comes up to him and puts her hands on his shoulders, and they begin a pas de deux.

Aurora and the Prince dance together, then Aurora moves around among the nymphs, with the Prince following her, before they come together again. Finally Aurora slips from the Prince's grasp and she disappears offstage, followed by the Prince. The nymphs dance in the forest, and then Aurora reappears to do a solo while they watch her. After another

Above: Aurora and the Prince dance their pas de deux.

Left: The Lilac Fairy and her nymphs watch as Aurora and the Prince dance together.

Below: Aurora's solo in the midst of the nymphs.

dance for the nymphs, joined eventually by Aurora, she pirouettes into the Prince's arms before leaving him once more and vanishing.

As she leaves, the nymphs cluster around the Prince and he, dazzled, believes that Aurora has simply vanished among them. When he tries to find her, the nymphs disappear, and he finds himself alone once more with the Lilac Fairy. "Where has she gone?" he asks.

"Follow me," the Lilac Fairy tells him.

Above: The nymphs enter and form patterns onstage, through which the Lilac Fairy leads Prince Florimund on his journey to Princess Aurora's castle. In some productions of this ballet, a magical ship appears and carries the Prince and the Lilac Fairy to the castle.

As the Prince nears the castle, Carabosse appears and tries to overcome him and make him turn back, but each time she starts to cast a spell, the Lilac Fairy intervenes and breaks it. The gauze curtains that formed the forest at the end of Act 1 disappear one by one and Prince Florimund begins to see the sleeping courtiers. Then he sees Princess Aurora asleep in her bower. Puzzled, he turns to the Lilac Fairy. "She's asleep! What should I do?"

"Think," she tells him.

"I shall kiss her," says the Prince. As he goes toward Aurora, Carabosse, who has crept into the sleeping court, tries to prevent him from touching her, but the Lilac Fairy's power is too great and Carabosse falls back. When Prince Florimund kisses Aurora she wakes up, and the whole court begins to stir into life once more. Defeated, Carabosse falls to the ground, dead. Prince Florimund and Princess Aurora stand hand in hand, surrounded by the awakened court as the curtain falls.

Left: Princess Aurora lies asleep.

Below: The Prince gives Aurora a kiss.

ACT 3

This whole act is devoted to the wedding of
Princess Aurora and Prince Florimund. Sometimes
this act is performed on its own, as a miniature ballet
called *Aurora's Wedding*. Many fairy-tale characters
come to celebrate the wedding.

Top: The court greets the King and Queen as they
make their entrance.

Bottom: The courtiers dance during the festivities.

Right: There are four *divertissements* at the wedding. The first is the *pas de quatre*. As well as dancing together, each dancer has a solo.

Below: The second divertissement — the White Cat and Puss-in-Boots. The White Cat is carried in on cushions held by four attendants.

Left: The third divertissement — the Bluebird and Princess Florine. This is one of the most famous pas de deux and is often performed on its own. Almost every well-known male dancer will have danced the role of Bluebird at some time in his career if he belongs to a company that does this ballet. The Bluebird and Princess Florine both have solos, but it is the Bluebird's solo that is outstanding. It is physically very demanding, and excellent technical skills are needed to dance it well.

Below: The fourth divertissement — Little Red Riding Hood and the Wolf. Together they act out their story. At the end, the Wolf carries Red Riding Hood, kicking and struggling, offstage.

After the divertissements, Prince Florimund and Princess Aurora dance together, watched by the court. Then it is time for the final dance, in which the courtiers and the fairy-tale characters join together. The King formally gives his daughter's hand in marriage to the Prince, and the Lilac Fairy gives the couple her blessing. The ballet ends with great rejoicing over the wedding.

Above: A classic pose from the grand pas de deux for the Prince and Princess at the end of Act 3.

Right: A fish dive from the grand pas de deux. This is the movement being rehearsed in the studio on page 11.

CURTAIN CALLS

Curtain calls are organized beforehand; everyone has a particular place to stand. The first call is for the whole company, and maybe, if there is a lot of applause, the second and third calls as well. Then those members of the corps de ballet without solo parts take their call, followed by those who have danced solos, starting with the smallest roles and ending with the main characters: Carabosse and the Lilac Fairy, followed by Prince Florimund and Princess Aurora. Aurora brings the conductor of the orchestra onstage to take his bow, and the conductor, in turn, introduces the members of the orchestra, who take their bow from the orchestra pit.

The Sleeping Beauty lasts for three hours, so it is 10:30 or 11:00 p.m. when the curtain falls for the last time. The dancers go back to their dressing rooms, take off their costumes and makeup, and perhaps have a shower. They check the notice board to see which rehearsals they must attend the following day, and then go off in search of something to eat. Dancers rarely have their dinner before a performance, because it is very uncomfortable to dance on a full stomach. If they are in their home theater, they can go home for dinner, but if they are on tour, it can be very hard to find any food so late at night.

For many dancers, the day does not end here. Certain chores, such as washing practice clothes and sewing shoes, still have to be done before they can finally collapse into bed. It's important to get a good night's rest, because tomorrow it all begins again.

Above: The final pose as the curtain falls.

Top: The cast acknowledges the applause of the audience.

Above: Dancers often receive flowers after a performance. They are either presented onstage or left with the stage-door keeper, as here.

Left: Still wearing his makeup, a dancer checks the next day's rehearsal schedule on the notice board.

THE STORY OF THE SLEEPING BEAUTY BALLET

The Sleeping Beauty is one of the five great classical ballets, the other four being *Swan Lake*, *The Nutcracker*, *Coppélia*, and *Giselle*. Classical ballets are characterized by their difficult dance arrangements for the corps de ballet, and by their pas de deux, which are often accompanied by male and female solos specially choreographed to show off the skills of the dancers.

Like many classical ballets, *The Sleeping Beauty* was created at the Imperial Russian Ballet in St. Petersburg. In the nineteenth century, this ballet company, which was paid for by the czar, frequently employed French choreographers. One of these was Marius Petipa (1819–1910), the chief ballet master from 1869 to 1903, who created some of the finest classical ballets, including *The Sleeping Beauty*. The music for the ballet was written by the Russian composer Peter Ilich Tchaikovsky (1840–93), who also wrote the music for *Swan Lake* and *The Nutcracker*.

The first performance of *The Sleeping Beauty* was at the Maryinsky Theater of Saint Petersburg in 1890. Although it was not an instant success, it did eventually become a favorite with audiences, and it has been performed regularly in Russia and many other countries ever since.

Margot Fonteyn and Rudolf Nureyev as Princess Aurora and Prince Florimund.

The dancer who created the role of Aurora for the Imperial Russian ballet was an Italian ballerina, Carlotta Brianza (1867–1935). Another Italian dancer, Enrico Cecchetti (1850–1928) created the roles of both Carabosse and Bluebird. Mathilde Kschessinskaya (1872–1971) was the first Russian Aurora. The famous Russian ballerina Anna Pavlova (1882–1931) also danced the role. It was when Anna Pavlova was taken to see this ballet as a very young girl that she resolved to become a dancer and one day perform the role of Aurora herself — an ambition that she achieved in 1908.

British dancers Margot Fonteyn (1919–91) and Alicia Markova (b.1910) have been outstanding in the role of Aurora, which has also been danced to great acclaim by Canadian Karen Kain (b.1951), American Gelsey Kirkland (b.1953) and Russian Irina Kolpakova (b.1933). More recent famous Auroras include Japanese Miyako Yoshida (b.1965), who dances with the Birmingham Royal Ballet Company in England, and American Darci Kistler (b.1964), who dances with the New York City Ballet. Australian dancer Robert Helpmann (1909–86) was the most famous Carabosse, and Russian-born Rudolf Nureyev (1938–93) and Yuri Soloviev (1940–77) were two of the best-known Bluebirds.

Theatre Museum, V & A

Robert Helpmann as Carabosse.

46

GLOSSARY

Note: All ballet companies are made up of dancers with different levels of experience and ability. Generally speaking, there are three major levels: the corps de ballet, the soloists, and the principals. However, ballet companies have different structures, and sometimes they classify dancers by other names. For example, a female principal dancer is sometimes known as a ballerina.

Most ballet steps have French names, because the basic ones were invented at the dancing school founded by Louis XIV of France in 1661. Every step in ballet is based on one of seven movements: bending (*plié*), stretching (*tendu*), sliding (*glissé*), rising (*relevé*), darting (*élancé*), jumping (*sauté*), and turning (*tourné*).

Arabesque A position in which the dancer lifts one leg off the ground and stretches it out straight behind. There are several different types of arabesques with different arm and body positions.

Attitude A position in which the dancer lifts one leg off the ground and bends it at the knee, either behind or in front of the body.

Ballet Master / Ballet Mistress In most companies, the person in charge of rehearsals, who often teaches in the company ballet classes as well.

Character Part A part such as Carabosse in *The Sleeping Beauty* that is usually physically less demanding than a principal role such as Aurora, but needs skilled interpretation and dramatic ability.

Choreography The art of creating a ballet by composing sequences of steps to be danced to music. A person who creates ballets is called a **choreographer**. Most ballet companies use systems of special symbols known as dance notation to write down the steps so that they are not forgotten.

Corps de ballet The large group of dancers who act as a "chorus" in the ballet, doing the big group dances. In *The Sleeping Beauty*, for example, the corps plays the parts of fairies, courtiers, and wedding guests. The dancers in the rank above the corps are known as **coryphées** and they often go on to become soloists. However, coryphées still dance with the corps when required. Most dancers begin their career in the corps before going on to dance smaller solo parts such as Red Riding Hood or the Wolf in the divertissement in Act 3 of *The Sleeping Beauty*.

Divertissement A short dance such as Red Riding Hood and the Wolf's in Act 3 of *The Sleeping Beauty* or the Spanish dance in Act 2 of *The Nutcracker*, performed by a small number of people, usually at a point in the ballet when there is a break in the plot.

Grand jeté A great, dramatic leap through the air with the legs outstretched.

On pointe Danced on the tips of the toes, wearing block-toed pointe shoes.

Pas de deux A dance for two people. The French phrase means "steps for two." A **pas de quatre** is a dance for four people.

Pirouette A turning or spinning step.

Principals Dancers who perform the leading roles in ballets, such as Princess Aurora and Prince Florimund in *The Sleeping Beauty*.

Rosin An amber-colored crystal which is made from the sap of pine trees. When dancers rub their shoes in the crushed or powdered crystal, a layer of rosin dust coats the soles and keeps the dancers from slipping.

Soloists (from the word *solo* meaning "alone") Dancers who perform by themselves in important roles. For example, in *The Sleeping Beauty*, the parts of the six fairies who come to present gifts at Aurora's christening may be danced by soloists. Soloists do not necessarily dance leading roles, but a senior soloist may be given some of the less physically demanding ones such as Prince Florimund.